I0233536

NOW

THE URGENCY AND THE KEY
TO REACH THIS GENERATION
WITH THE MESSAGE OF CHRIST

NOW

The Urgency and the Key to reach this generation with the message of Christ

© 2015 JA Pérez

All rights reserved. This book contains material protected under International and Federal Copyright Laws and Treaties. Any unauthorized reprint or use of this material is prohibited. No part of this book may be reproduced or transmitted in any form or by any means, electronic or mechanical, including photocopying, recording, or by any information storage and retrieval system without express written permission from the publisher.

For permission requests, write to the publisher, addressed "Attention: Permissions Coordinator," at the address below.

P.O. Box211325
Chula Vista, CA 91921 USA

Scripture quotations marked (NLT) are taken from the Holy Bible, NEW LIVING TRANSLATION, copyright © 1996, 2004, 2007 by Tyndale House Foundation. Used by permission of Tyndale House Publishers, Inc., Carol Stream, Illinois 60188. All rights reserved.

Scripture quotations marked (NIV) are taken from THE HOLY BIBLE, NEW INTERNATIONAL VERSION®, NIV® Copyright © 1973, 1978, 1984, 2011 by Biblica, Inc.® Used by permission. All rights reserved worldwide.

Scripture quotations marked (NRSV) are from the NEW REVISED STANDARD VERSION Bible, copyright © 1989 the Division of Christian Education of the National Council of the Churches of Christ in the United States of America. Used by permission. All rights reserved.

Unless otherwise noted, all other biblical references are quoted from King James Version version of the Bible. The KJV is public domain in the United States.

Published by: Keen Sight Books
www.KeenSightBooks.com

Report errors to errata@keensightbooks.com

ISBN: 978-0692411612

Printed in the U.S.A.

What others are saying...

This could be a prototype for the future! —*Dr. Jaime Mirón, General Editor of the NTV (Spanish translation of the Bible)*

JA Pérez models effective collaboration... bringing together ministries with shared goals, values, and complementary gifts to positively impact cities. —*David L. Jones, Vice President of Corporate Affairs / Luis Palau Association*

JA Pérez has come up with something—that every outreach facilitator needs—extremely important and essential for the work of the Kingdom. —*Alpha Hayward, Senior/Founding Pastor of Revolution Foursquare Church*

We are grateful to the JA Pérez Association for bringing the festival to our city... the effects of the event will stay in the city long after the project has concluded with an extended impact reaching over 80,000 people. —*Pastor José Ramón Alvarado, Festival Committee Member*

When the JA Pérez Team comes into an area... they are not there to put on a "show", they go with every intention of making a permanent impact in the name of Jesus! —*Georgina Verzal, Evangelist/Founder of Reg3neration™*

JA Pérez has implemented a model of collaboration for evangelists that benefits all involved. Whether your ministry is well seasoned or starting up, there's a place for you to serve, learn, and build God's kingdom together. —*Paul Durham, Evangelist/President, Ripe 4 Life Ministries*

JA Pérez understands the value of working together in collaboration and the power that comes when sisters and brothers serve together to love God and love people. —*Jeff Pieper, Director of Strategic Relationships / Luis Palau Association*

(a full list of testimonials on page 129)

Contents

Acknowledgements

I would like to express my gratitude to the people who saw me through this work; to all those who talked things over, read, offered comments, allowed me to quote their remarks and assisted in the editing, proofreading and design.

To my wife Anabel, my sons Sam and Jesse and my daughter Amy who always support me when I write, in spite of all the time it takes me away from them.

To my mother Tere for helping me with the proofreading and revisions.

I would also like to thank all my mentors—some already in our heavenly home and others still teaching me life lessons.

Last but not least: A special thanks to my cat "Link" who sleeps on my desk and keeps me company while I write.

PART I

The Urgency

CHAPTER 1

Only One Generation Away

Freedom is never more than one generation away from extinction. —Ronald Reagan

The records show several revivals in the history of the Church. Special times when the word of God penetrated every level of society resulting in great awakenings. Of course you cannot save everyone, but the vast majority of the population in the old and new world was well evangelized. Churches got full, nations abandoned practices of immorality, and human dignity was elevated. In times like that, Christians celebrated with great expectancy the reality that Christ could and would return on their days as they could almost say: *"This generation has been reached."*

But then, a new generation would rise.

In Egypt, the children of Israel experienced a great season of blessings under Joseph's leadership, but when he died, a new generation arose, and this generation did not know Joseph nor the God of Joseph.

> *Now there arose up a new king over Egypt, which knew not Joseph. Exodus 1:8 (KJV)*

That's right. A new generation comes in, and this generation does not know God.

The work of evangelism must go on, for when you think you have reached a whole generation, a new one is born.

Paul had reached his generation.

He says in Romans:

> *I have fully presented the Good News of Christ from Jerusalem all the way to Illyricum. Romans 15:19*

I like the way it reads in the Spanish Reina Valera 1960 Version.

It says: *"desde Jerusalén, y por los alrededores hasta Ilírico, todo lo he llenado del evangelio de Cristo,"* which directly translates: *"From Jerusalem and all over, all the way to Illyricum, I have filled it all up with the gospel of Christ."*

Paul's message and influence penetrated all levels of society across the roman empire. And this empire extended to almost all their known world at that time.

Then... one generation later, we see some of the churches leaving the teachings of Paul and falling into false doctrines.

Asia Minor is one example of this.

Paul was still around when those churches abandoned him and his teachings of grace.

> *As you know, everyone from the province of Asia has deserted me—even Phygelus and Hermogenes.* 2 Timothy 1:15 (NLT)

Later—before the end of the century—we see the condition of these churches in Asia when John wrote to them in the book of Revelation.

On the second century, Ignatius—the bishop of Antioch in Syria—was arrested and sent to Rome under armed guard. Ignatius traveled (some believe by ship) from Antioch to the southern coast of Asia Minor and passed through Philadelphia, then traveled to Smyrna where he got to know Polycarp, the bishop of Smyrna and where he was visited by Christians from Ephesus, Magnesia, and Tralles, whom he had contacted to inform them of his journey.

He then went on to Troas, and from there wrote to the churches of Philadelphia and Smyrna and also to Polycarp.

Ignatius wrote about one group of opponents in the churches of Western Asia Minor and that they were what he calls Judaizing Gnostics. The identity of the opponents is significant with regard to discussion about the origin and development of Gnosticism. Ignatius also faced Judaizers in Magnesia and

Philadelphia, and docetists in Tralles and Smyrna. Scholars (like Hengel[1]) say that docetism is the result of what some call *"the first Hellenization of Christianity."*

So, as the churches in Asia Minor received the good news by the preaching of Paul and a generation later got infiltrated by false teachings, paganism and immorality; it is the same in our time.

As you see, no matter how good of a job we did in bringing the good news to the previous generation... a new generation is now here, and we must do the work of evangelism all over again.

Our history is full of cycles like that.

There was a time in the United States, when one evangelist was called to the White House to pray for the president. Billy Graham blessed the inauguration of many presidents.

Prayer was allowed and encouraged in public schools and school textbooks used to mention God.

But those days are gone.

Our current President has proclaimed that *"we are no longer a Christian nation, at least not just[2]."*

"Now there arose up a new king over Egypt, which knew not Joseph."

We have work to do. Here is a whole new generation that

14

does not know God.

We must reach it. It is "urgent" for if we don't reach it, we might lose the one after, and the one after that one.

There is an urgency.

CHAPTER 2

Current World Status

Has everyone heard?

One sometimes hears the comment *"Certainly most everyone has heard of Jesus by now. Surely missionaries have been sent to every country. Haven't we already completed the Great Commission?"* While the spread of Christianity has been nothing short of supernatural, there are still huge segments of the world's population that have never heard the name of Jesus let alone a clear presentation of the message of salvation.

People groups

> *Go therefore and make disciples of every nation*
> *[people group]. - Jesus (Matthew 28:19)*

To map correctly the number of unreached people I'll be using the terms *"people"*, *"people group"* and *"ethnic people"* synonymously using the Lausanne Committee guidelines[3].

What is a people group?

A significantly large grouping of individuals who perceive

themselves to have a common affinity with one another. *"For evangelization purposes, a people group is the largest group within which the Gospel can spread as a church planting movement without encountering barriers of understanding or acceptance."*

In many parts of the world lack of understandability serves as the main barrier and it is appropriate to define people groups primarily by language with the possibility of sub-divisions based on dialect or cultural variations.

In other parts of the world, most notably in portions of South Asia, acceptance is a greater barrier than understandability. In these regions, caste, religious tradition, location, common histories and legends, plus language may be used to define the boundaries of each people group[4].

There are 11,243 people groups in the world (7 billion people) and 6,543 unreached people groups (4 billion people[5]).

Here are some sobering facts about just the 50 largest unreached people groups[6]:

- All 50 of these people groups have less than 2% Christ-followers.

- Individuals in these groups have very limited, if any, access to the Gospel.

- One in five people on earth live in these 50

unreached peoples.

- These 50 unreached people groups are comprised of 1.365 billion souls.

- Every group is larger than 10,000,000 in population.

- None have an indigenous church capable of taking the Gospel to the entire group.

- Primary religion: 22 are Muslim, 18 Hindu, 5 Buddhist, 3 Ethnic Religions, 1 non-Religious, 1 Sikh.

- 46 of these 50 unreached people groups are in the 10/40 Window, 43 are in closed countries.

The 10/40 Window

The 10/40 Window[7] is the rectangular area of North Africa, the Middle East and Asia approximately between 10 degrees and 40 degrees north latitude. *The 10/40 Window* is often called *"The Resistant Belt"* and includes the majority of the world's Muslims, Hindus, and Buddhists. The original 10/40 Window included only countries with at least 50% of their land mass within 10 and 40 degrees north latitude. *The revised 10/40 Window* includes several additional countries, such as Indonesia, that are close to 10 or 40 degrees north latitude and have high concentrations of unreached peoples.

An estimated 4.75 billion individuals residing in approximately 8,366 distinct people groups are in the revised

10/40 Window.

The 10/40 Window is home to some of the largest unreached people groups in the world such as the Shaikh, Yadava, Turks, Moroccan Arabs, Pashtun, Jat and Burmese.

Historical and Biblical Significance

The first and most fundamental reason why followers of Jesus Christ ought to focus on the 10/40 Window is because of the Biblical and historical significance of this area. The Bible begins with the account of Adam and Eve placed by God in the heart of what is now the 10/40 Window.

God's plan, expressed in Genesis 1:26, was that mankind should have dominion over the earth, subduing it fully. However, Adam and Eve sinned against God and forfeited their right to rule. Man's sinful behavior increased until God intervened and judged the earth with a cataclysmic flood.

Then came man's futile attempt to establish new dominion in the building of the great Tower of Babel. That effort, which also occurred in the heart of the 10/40 Window, was an open defiance against God. Once again, God reached forth His hand in judgment. The result was the introduction of different languages, the scattering of earth's people, and the formation of nations.

The Least Evangelized Countries

The 10/40 Window is home to the majority of the world's

unevangelized countries. The *"unevangelized"* are people who have a minimal knowledge of the gospel, but have no valid opportunity to respond to it. While it constitutes only one-third of earth's total land area, nearly two-thirds of the world's people reside in the 10/40 Window.

As I mentioned before, the original 10/40 Window included only countries with at least 50% of their land mass within 10 and 40 degrees north latitude and the revised 10/40 Window removes several Christianized countries such as South Korea and the Philippines and includes several additional countries, such as Indonesia, that are close to 10 or 40 degrees north latitude and have high concentrations of unreached peoples. These countries include both sovereign states and non-sovereign dependencies.

The Unreached Peoples and Cities

An estimated 2.91 billion individuals live in approximately 5,840 unreached people groups are in the 10/40 Window. The 10/40 Window also contains the largest unreached peoples over one million. In addition, the 10/40 Window contains the overwhelming majority of the world's least evangelized megacities—that is those with a population of more than one million.

The top 50 least evangelized megacities are all in the 10/40 Window. That fact alone underscores the need for prioritizing 10/40 Window Great Commission efforts.

The Dominance of Three Religious Blocs

The 10/40 Window contains four of the world's dominant religious blocs.

The majority of the followers of Islam, Hinduism, and Buddhism as well as the Non-Religious bloc live within the 10/40 Window.

On the left side or western part of the 10/40 Window, the Muslim world can be seen most prominently in a wide band across the north of Africa into the Middle East.

South Asia, in the middle of the 10/40 Window, is the heart of Hinduism with its 330 million gods. Buddhism influences the right side or eastern part of the 10/40 Window.

Buddhism is the primary religion in Southeast Asia and although officially an atheistic country since the Marxist revolution of the late 1940s, China is nevertheless deeply influenced by its Buddhist roots.

The Preponderance of the Poor

The 10/40 Window is home to the majority of the world's poor. Of the poorest of the poor, more than eight out of ten live in the 10/40 Window. On average, they exist on less than a few hundred dollars per person per year.

It has been said that *"the poor are the lost, and the lost are the poor"* as the majority of the unreached live in the poorest countries of the world. There is a remarkable overlap between the poorest countries of the world and those that are least evangelized.

A Renewed Focus

The focus of the Christian missions community 200 years ago was for the coastlands of the world. A century later, the success of the coastlands effort motivated a new generation to reach the interior regions of the continents.

Within the past several decades, the success of the inland thrust has led to a major focus on people groups. Today, followers of Christ are concentrating their efforts on the unreached peoples of the world, most of which are in the 10/40 Window.

Our Continent

North America and the Caribbean

The 30 countries in North America and the Caribbean include three of the largest countries of the world: Canada, USA and Greenland. Communities from every ethnic group in Europe have settled in the Americas.

It is probably the region with the least religious discrimination and it has been the largest sending base in the world for missionaries but that is rapidly changing. Eighty-three least-reached people groups remain here.

Canada has the largest percent of population that is least-reached with 4.6% in 16 groups (nearly 1.5 million people) but the United States has the largest population of least-reached people at over 3.5 million in 24 people groups.

Mexico has almost 5 million in 18 people groups. If the gospel is not sent, sometimes people come to hear the gospel in a land where churches are plentiful. This could be the legacy of North American Christianity.

Students, immigrant communities, and indigenous peoples remain a challenge for the gospel in this the world's wealthiest continent and the economic engine on which the world's economy depends for growth. Less than 15% of international students in the US today are touched by any Christian ministry.

In addition, 70% will never see the inside of an American home and 80% will never have a Christian friend. And, it's ironic that American churches pray for Muslim countries but do very little to reach Muslims in their own communities. Perhaps we are unaware of their presence or we do not know how to build bridges of friendship to share good news.

In addition, only in Greenland are Native Americans a majority; elsewhere they are often a marginalized underclass alongside a large majority that overran their continent.

Pray for re-energizing the Body of Christ in North America and the Caribbean to come alongside the rapidly emerging harvest forces from China, Russia, Latin America, India,

Africa, and other places... peoples joining together to glorify God among all peoples[8].

Central and South America

"God, gold and glory" was the rallying cry of the Spaniards who went to the New World. God was the motivator for many Jesuit missionaries, and that put them in conflict with those who came to take the gold and enslave those who needed God.

The original inhabitants were decimated by european conquests and diseases in the 16th and 19th centuries. In 1900, almost the entire Spanish-speaking population was considered Catholic but since then, changes have been dramatic—from narrow traditionalism with strong opposition to Protestant activity to freedom of religion and a rapid growth of Evangelicals.

Spiritism has grown rapidly in influence in many countries. The divinely ordered convergence in Latin America of greater freedom of religion, more open and accountable democracy, a series of military, natural and economic disasters which loosened the hold of traditional structures enabled many to come to Christ.

Today there has been a rapid growth and maturation of missions' vision which has sparked numerous initiatives to the unreached. Among the 21 countries in Central and South America, 97 least-reached peoples remain, from the 50.9% of the population of Guyana in 5 least-reached groups to the

15.4% of Brazil's population in 46 different people groups, to the more than 600,000 Jews in Argentina, their remaining least-reached people[9].

Author's Note:

(Before you read the next chapter)

If you are a millennial reading this book, I understand that the fact that I'm categorizing your generation as a group, might be offensive and interpreted as stereotyping. I assure you that it is not my intention to be critical or disrespectful of your generation by using apparent generalizations.

The characteristics noted here are for the purpose of making the sharing of the *Good News* relevant to the smarter and most informed generation that has ever existed.

CHAPTER 3

The Millennials

I have written in other works about the need to always adapt the models we use to the present generation. Although the message of the Gospel has been the same for 2000 years, the models (the way and the tools we use to present it) must be relevant to each generation and group. I will touch more on this at a later chapter.

The apostle Paul understood this. That's why he opened his address to the Athenians on Mars' Hill with a few poignant remarks about *"the Unknown God"* instead of launching straightway into a five-point sermon on sin and salvation (Acts 17:22-31). He had something similar in view when he wrote, *"I have become all things to all men, that I might by all means save some"* (I Corinthians 9:22).

The days of long sermonizing messages are gone. The same as the old fire and brimstones fear-striking preaching that for decades manipulated uneducated audiences into religion and the keeping of men-imposed rules and ascetic practices. Not even poetic oratoria has the effect that it used to in years passed when the masses were hypnotized by the great charisma of a famous speaker.

Not anymore dear reader. Those days are gone... and I'm glad.

We are in the presence of a new generation. More educated and with access to a lot more information than what our parents used to have.

Welcome the Millennials

They will not be seduced by any of the above mentioned religious practices, but they will value authenticity. Millennials want authenticity.

Who are they?

They are now the largest generational demographic, subsuming the place of priority long held by the Baby Boomers[10]. In the US, the millennial generation, roughly defined as people born from 1980 to 2004, is now estimated to number 80 million, making it a larger group than the Boomers.

Since the 1950s and the rise of teen subculture as a marketing demographic, the Baby Boomers, people born from 1946 to 1964, have dominated culture and consumerism in America. This all came about because of the post-World War II baby boom. When military men returned from the war to an increasingly affluent America and started families, they produced the largest generation in history—and the largest demographic—until now. But now its reign is over. Long live the Millennials!

The term *"millennials"* goes back to the late 1980s, when the Millennials were first entering school. Authors William Strauss and Neil Howe are credited with coining the term. They discussed them in the book *"Generations: The History of America's Future[11]"* and later wrote an entire book about them, called *"Millennials Rising: The Next Great Generation."*

The Millennials grew up during a period of profound technological advances that changed the environment in which people grew up. Starting with the PC at the beginning of the Millennials' lifespan, and evolving to the Internet and smartphones, technology has created an unprecedented shift in the environment in which human behavior is molded.

Virtually everyone with a message must now come to terms with Millennials, who they are and what they like.

Here are some varying and sometimes seemingly contradictory tips from the field of a very inexact science.

Brent Green, author of "Marketing to Leading Edge Baby Boomers[12]" said, *"They're well traveled when compared to older generations, so they have sophisticated sensibilities about what is authentic versus fake, and they prefer the former."*

Green also said, *"They value and need online engagement with social networks because their travel experiences must be shared with peers in real time whenever possible[13]."*

Outside the US

The influence of Millennials worldwide

A new study was issued (interviewing 4,000 Millennials in 11 countries) to better understand the evolving roles of brands in Millennials' lives and how cultural changes like the global recession are impacting their behaviors[14].

The study shows the way Millennials perceive their lives and future.

The global recession has fundamentally changed Millennials.

The economy is a key factor in Millennials' lives and within their community. In fact, economic stability is the number one hope that Millennials have for their country. The troubling job market also has created a new breed of Millennial entrepreneurs, with 48 percent of Millennials saying that owning their own business is a top life goal (76 percent in Turkey and 65 percent in Brazil).

Millennials are alpha-influencers: Seven in ten believe it is their responsibility to share feedback when they have a good or bad experience.

When we reach Millennials with the message of Christ, we need to keep in mind we are engaging with this new breed of entrepreneurs and world leaders.

As evangelists, we need to present our message using smart models. We need to be precise, and make sense.

Michele Serro says, [Millennials] are extremely impatient with irrelevant information, and they have no tolerance for unwieldy experiences[15].

How to reach Millennials?

Millennials are different. Millennials want authenticity.

They will not be seduced by impressive oratoria or imposed religious practices, but they will value authenticity.

In part two of this book, I will talk about the things we need to keep in mind when reaching millennials.

CHAPTER 4

The Urgency

Time is our most precious commodity. We only get a certain amount of it and then it's gone forever.

This is not only true in things concerning our own personal lives—we all have goals and dreams we want to achieve and understand time is limited—this is also important concerning evangelism.

Urgency is not a technique like the one a salesperson would use when trying to close a deal—a salesperson would tell you something like *"the special offer expires today, so you must buy it now."*

When it comes to evangelism, urgency is real.

Yes, a sense of urgency is a driving force behind personal evangelism and without it evangelism loses one of it's core motivations, but this urgency is real and it has a strong biblical foundation.

And this gospel of the kingdom shall be

preached in all the world for a witness unto all nations; and then shall the end come.
Matthew 24:14 (KJV)

We only have a time frame in which to reach a generation.

Time goes by fast.

The End is Near

It comes to mind the image of a street preacher holding a sign that says *"the end is near"*, screaming a hell and brimstone message out of his lungs.

Some listeners passing by will feel convicted and afraid and will proceed to answer the call—with true repentance or because of the need to calm their guilt. Others will simply think he is crazy.

Still, the text is there. Jesus said: *"And this gospel of the kingdom shall be preached in all the world for a witness unto all nations; and then shall the end come."*

The end of what?

Most theologians agree that Jesus was not prophesying a catastrophic destruction of the globe, where the whole planet explodes, and that's it.

If you read the context, Jesus was answering three questions to his disciples.

34

First, the conversation is about the city of Jerusalem.

> *And Jesus went out, and departed from the temple: and his disciples came to him for to shew him the buildings of the temple. And Jesus said unto them, See ye not all these things? verily I say unto you, There shall not be left here one stone upon another, that shall not be thrown down. Matthew 24:1,2 (KJV)*

So the first prophecy in this chapter is that: *"There (in Jerusalem) shall not be left here one stone upon another..."*

Now, right after the prophecy, the disciples ask him three questions(v.3):

1- When shall these things be?

2- What shall be the sign of thy coming? and

3- Of the end of the world?

> *And as He sat upon the mount of Olives, the disciples came unto him privately, saying, Tell us, when shall these things be? and what shall be the sign of thy coming, and of the end of the world? Matthew 24:3 (KJV)*

Then Jesus answered to his disciples giving them a list of signs pointing to the end to answer the first question.

Some of these signs would include: False Christs, wars and

rumours of wars, nation will rise against nation, kingdom against kingdom, famines, pestilences, earthquakes, etc...

> *And Jesus answered and said unto them, Take heed that no man deceive you. For many shall come in my name, saying, I am Christ; and shall deceive many. And ye shall hear of wars and rumours of wars: see that ye be not troubled: for all these things must come to pass, but the end is not yet. For nation shall rise against nation, and kingdom against kingdom: and there shall be famines, and pestilences, and earthquakes, in divers places... Matthew 24:4,7 (KJV)*

Then Jesus answer the second question *"what shall be the sign of thy coming."*

> *Immediately after the tribulation of those days shall the sun be darkened, and the moon shall not give her light, and the stars shall fall from heaven, and the powers of the heavens shall be shaken: And then shall appear the sign of the Son of man in heaven: and then shall all the tribes of the earth mourn, and they shall see the Son of man coming in the clouds of heaven with power and great glory. Matthew 24:29,30 (KJV)*

In more detail, the Lord says how He comes: *"All the tribes of the earth shall see the Son of man coming in the clouds of heaven"* and what happens when he comes *"And he shall send his angels with a great sound of a trumpet, and they shall gather together his elect from the four winds, from one end of heaven to the other" (v.31).*

Praise God. When he comes back he will *"gather together his elect"*, that's us. Any follower of Jesus who is alive when he returns.

There are different schools of interpretation when it comes to the timing of this rapture. Some believe it will happen before the great tribulation Jesus mentioned in verse 21st of this chapter. Others believe it will happen in the middle and others at the end of the great tribulation.

I will not get into eschatological details in this book as my assignment is more to talk about the urgency of preaching the good news to this generation rather than doctrinal, but one thing is clear—independently of to what school of though you belong to regarding the timing of the rapture—Jesus is coming back.

We don't know the day or the hour, but we know He is coming back, and that creates urgency.

We don't know if He is coming in this generation, but if He does, we have the responsibility to reach it before that day comes.

You might ask: What if He doesn't come in this generation?

We still have to reach it because it's a mandate.

> *Therefore, go and make disciples of all the nations, baptizing them in the name of the Father and the Son and the Holy Spirit. Matthew 28:19 (NLT)*

But, believe me. There is an urgency.

> *And this gospel of the kingdom shall be preached in all the world for a witness unto all nations; and then shall the end come. Matthew 24:14 (KJV)*

So my friend, you might be an evangelist or perhaps, just a follower of Christ.

Here are two things we have to keep in front of our eyes so we don't get distracted:

1- We have a mandate.

2- Time is limited.

Using time wisely

Lets use our time wisely, keeping in mind that sharing the good news should be a priority in our daily lives.

Apostle Paul tell the Ephesians not to waste time.

> *Redeeming the time, because the days are evil...* *Ephesians 5:16 (KJV)*

38

The NLT translates the first part of the text like this: *"Make the most of every opportunity."*

Evangelism as a way of life

As we make sharing the good news a priority in our daily schedules, it is my prayer that you and I learn to be ready for when an opportunity presents itself.

I teach this simple concept in one of our *Effective Evangelism*™ leadership seminars in Latin America. We call this principle *"Evangelism as a way of life."*

This is what Paul tells Timothy:

> *Preach the word of God. Be prepared, whether the time is favorable or not... 2 Timothy 4:2 (NLT)*

PART II

The Key

CHAPTER 5

A Change Of Strategy

The key to reach this generation with the message of Christ is collaboration.

Evangelism is not the work of one man.

I understand that's a big statement, and that's why I will layout for you in this second part of the book the principles that support this statement.

Reposition

The methods of western missions have to change—because global geopolitics have changed[16].

It was 1964, when Dr. John Edmund Haggai was in Beirut, Lebanon, on his first visit to West Asia, meeting with christian leaders from the region.

He was surprised to find them critical of local missionaries. That, frankly, made him angry. He told them what a crucial role the missionaries had played in his father's family coming to faith in Christ. He knew that missionaries the world over had sacrificed greatly, many giving their lives. How could anyone question the methods of those willing to pay such a high price for their commitment?

The local leaders replied to him, "No, no, no, habibi (habibi is an Arabic term of endearment), please don't be upset. But the truth is, people of high intellect and high position here are not willing to let young foreigners set the agenda, deploy the leadership personnel, and, in short, call the shots. They aren't rejecting Jesus. They're rejecting western domination and philosophical colonialism[17]." The conditions underlying two hundred years of missionary endeavors had been blown away in the aftermath of World War II.

That is one of the basic truths we have to keep in mind when we travel to nations and to the different ethnic groups to bring to them the good news. *"People of high intellect and high position—in those countries—are not willing to let young foreigners set the agenda."*

That is why it's necessary to re-think the models and ways in which we do missionary evangelism.

Rebranding Evangelism

I'm a firm believer in the need to restore the integrity and dignity of the office of the evangelist.

Many damages have been done in the name of evangelism.

From abuses of power to the misuse of finances, to all

44

the scandals surrounding evangelists in the last century[18]. Many people have been hurt and when they hear a known evangelist is coming to their city, the wall of untrust and resentment rises.

To help overcome that, we have had to put in place certain measures when we come to do a city-wide evangelistic event.

For example, we make clear to the pastors that we will not raise offerings at the event, all services, assistance and event concerts are free. And we make it clear that the churches don't have to make any type of financial commitment to be a part of the event.

We have also integrated the national leaders not only in the ministering side of each project, but also in the decision making process during the logistics and preparations.

As they take ownership and become an essential part of the project, good things begin to happen.

When the pastors see that we don't have an agenda, other that bringing the message of Christ to those that don't know him, they lower that wall.

In the past few years, we have been able to establish good relations and work together with the nationals and many have come to hear the good news as a result of this change in philosophy.

The office of the evangelist is alive and well in the 21st century,

45

although the models and practices when it comes to "the how" of bringing the message, have had to be re-assessed and re-designed becoming more relevant to a whole new generation of unreached people.

Collaboration at the center

As followers of Christ, called to preach the good news "to all nations" and seeing how the mission's terrain has changed.

It is imperative that we adapt to new forms and methods—relevant and practical—to be able to reach the generation in front of us.

As I will detail later in the book, collaboration is at the center of everything we do to bring the message of Christ to every city, town and village where opportunity comes.

Yes, together we can reach more.

Not only by building strategic alliances among evangelists, but also joining efforts with leaders from every developing world culture. Leaders that already have access, stature, influence, and crucial knowledge of their local environments.

In the following pages we'll exhibit the practices that make a collaborative venture succeed in a culturally-sensitive world.

Using common sense and a minimalist approach, I will present core principles of partnership to help us accomplish the biblical mandate to reach the world for Christ. Why 50% of something is better than 100% of nothing. Bad practices in collaboration. Why collaboration is the way to do mass evangelism in the 21st century and much more.

CHAPTER 6

Principles Of Collaboration

Many seek the favor of the generous, and everyone is a friend to a giver of gifts.
Proverbs 19:6 (NRSV)

After reading the title for this chapter, you would have probably expected me to open it with a text that talks about working together, teamwork, or something of the sort. If one thing I have learned about collaboration is that "generosity" is probably that main force fueling any attempt to come work together.

Harvard professor Nicholas Christakis[19], co-author of *"Connected: The Surprising Power of Our Social Networks and How They Shape Our Lives[20]"* in a research, required participants to play a collaboration-testing game over the Internet. The obvious benefit of this approach is that it attracted a much larger sample than is traditionally the case for laboratory research. Courtesy of Amazon's Mechanical Turk over 750 volunteers were signed up for the experiment.

Participants in the game are allocated points. During each

round of the game they can donate points to their neighbors if they wish, with each donation matched by the *"game."* Obviously if everyone donates equally then each player gets significantly richer as a result. As game theory suggests however, should a participant defect and not donate, they stand to gain significantly from the donations of others without giving up any of their own points, at least in the short term before people cotton on and stop playing their game.

The mechanics of the game saw it split into three distinct rule sets. The first saw players interacting with the same people all the time, therefore their historical behavior was known to the others. The second variation meanwhile players were randomly reshuffled at the end of each round, while the final variation 1/3 of the players were shuffled.

In each of the variations one player from each pair was reminded how the other had acted in the previous round, but only in the third variation could they act on this information and decide whether to play with their partner or ask for a new one. To add spice to the game, at the end all of the points people have attained were converted into actual money. This was done to ensure that participants played the game as realistically as possible.

In all versions of the game approximately 60% of players co-operated to begin with. In the first two variants however, this dropped significantly once the impact of free loaders began to hit home. Tit-for-tat was being played out and after a few rounds collaboration was massively hit, down to around 15% on average.

Obviously the first two variants however gave players no choice over their partner, but in the third they could act upon previous behavior. In this version of the game collaboration remained stable throughout the game as players simply chose not to participate with the free loaders. This simple feedback mechanism enabled the community to become smarter and for collaboration to survive.

The research found that not only were collaborators wealthier at the end of the game, they had also gained significantly more connections than the freeloaders. Perhaps not surprising in itself, but one ray of light emerged when the freeloaders, as a result of being shunned, began to change their behavior to a more collaborative approach.

Furthermore, as they were shunned, the defectors began to change their behavior. A defector's likelihood of switching to co-operation increased with the number of players who had broken links with him in the previous round. Unlike straightforward tit-for-tat, social retaliation was having a marked effect.

So, what lessons can we take from this for real world collaboration?

The research clearly shows that it pays to be generous. It wasn't merely the selfish that were punished in future rounds but also the stingy.

And that's probably the main ingredient of all collaborative efforts.

Generosity

As we, older evangelists take the role of mentoring this new generation of brilliant and talented young messengers of good news, it is important that we *"take less space[21]"* and allow them to come in and play key roles, but this is going to take a lot more than words.

It will take sharing, making opportunities available to others, and using our established relations in cities and countries to open platforms and new venues for the up and coming young evangelists.

Generosity: *(also called largess or largesse)* is the habit of giving without expecting anything in return. It can involve offering time, assets or talents[22]...

The Merriam-Webster definition of generosity is:

> *"The quality of being kind, understanding, and not selfish: the quality of being generous; especially: willingness to give money and other valuable things to others[23]."*

Generosity involves giving to others not just anything in abundance, but rather giving those things that are good for others.

Generosity always intends to enhance the true wellbeing of those to whom it gives.

More than just giving

There is a mystery about generosity.

If you see it with your human eyes you might think that you lose—position, recognition, resources—when you give away what you have to others. And yes, "true generosity is giving and not expecting anything back" but God that is wise and wants you to be well, always rewards the giver in ways we cannot explain.

Paul writing to the Corinthians puts it this way:

> *Remember this: Whoever sows sparingly will also reap sparingly, and whoever sows generously will also reap generously. 2 Corinthians 9:6 (NIV)*

Creating a legacy

What could be more gratifying to an accomplished man or woman of God, than to know that their work will go further than they can naturally reach or go on longer than the years they are allowed to serve on this earth?

You see, there is an interest involved in this. And yes, you could be generous having some interests—like building a legacy. That does not take away from generosity.

53

"Generosity, to be clear, is not identical to pure altruism, since people can be authentically generous in part for reasons that serve their own interests as well as those of others. Indeed, insofar as generosity is a virtue, to practice it for the good of others also necessarily means that doing so achieves one's own true, long–term good as well[24]."

Learn it from the old prophets

In a sense, in ministry we see how prophets in the Bible made provisions for others to take on the mission as they became older and knew that their earthly ministries were coming to an end. Call it *a successor, a spiritual son,* or by any other title that might apply.

When Moses was ready to pass on the responsibilities of his ministry, God told him to get Joshua ready to take on the mission.

> *The Lord replied, "Take Joshua son of Nun, who has the Spirit in him, and lay your hands on him. Present him to Eleazar the priest before the whole community, and publicly commission him to lead the people. Transfer some of your authority to him so the whole community of Israel will obey him. Numbers 27:18-20 (NLT)*

You see the same pattern with Elijah and Elisha.

When time got closer for Elijah to depart, he prepared Elisha to take on the mission. Elisha was faithful by staying close to his mentor prophet, and when Elijah was taken, he picked up the prophet's mantle.

> *He took up also the mantle of Elijah that fell from him, and went back, and stood by the bank of Jordan; And he took the mantle of Elijah that fell from him, and smote the waters, and said, Where is the Lord God of Elijah? and when he also had smitten the waters, they parted hither and thither: and Elisha went over.*
> *2 Kings 2: 13-14 (KJV)*

It is interesting that the phrase *"taking on the mantle*[25]*"* is still used today in corporate circles when referring to successors.

Now, I'm not saying that collaborating means passing on your ministry to a successor. I'm referring to *"generosity"* in general and how it applies when it comes to building a legacy.

Still, for those of us *"young ministers"* that are still far away from even talking about legacy, the same *"generosity principle"* applies if you are going to do anything that is greater than yourself.

There are other principles that will work together with and around generosity. Those are key characteristics of any successful collaboration effort.

55

Here are other good principles learned on the Nicholas Christakis[26] research:

Participation: You want to encourage participation from across your organization. As we've seen from the experiment, this could involve removing, or at least educating, people that don't act collaboratively.

Collective: As collaboration will involve taking relatively narrow perspectives and making them broad, you will need to help the group reach a consensus and then take action collectively on the decisions they make.

Transparency: Feedback and trust are essential elements of collaboration. Being transparent with information is crucial if that is to be achieved. Make sure that all debates are in the open and that the entire group has access to the latest information.

Independence: James Surowiecki emphasized the importance of independent thought in his book Wisdom of Crowds[27], so you'll need to ensure that group-think does not emerge and that people are thinking for themselves.

Persistence: You will need to be persistent in your application of these principles, to ensure that all content is kept within the community and easily accessible to all members.

Emergence: Remember that the point of mass collaboration is to achieve great results, so ensure you focus on the end goal rather than worrying about how it is achieved. You will need your collaborative community to set their own goals and objectives.

Bringing it home

How collaboration is key for reaching nations with the message of Christ.

Mutual support

You are no longer alone. This is probably one of the most important benefits I experimented when I became part of the *Luis Palau NGA*[28].

The itinerant evangelist can easily become isolated. The road can be lonely.

As an evangelist you don't fit in many areas of church life today. When church culture—especially in America—turns inward (our building, our community, our couples group, our singles group, our Sunday school class, our midweek Bible study); an evangelist whose vision turns outward (to missions, nations, other groups and cultures) can get exceedingly frustrated and sometimes even feel as an outsider.

It's interesting that despite the fact we work for the church, and through the church, we have seen how little the church community really knows about the office of the evangelist in America. That probably explains why an evangelist usually feels more welcomed and appreciated by the churches in a foreign land than by our home churches.

Allow me to say that this might not be the case with the church where you and your family congregate, and I praise God for that (please stay there), but it sure is the case with many churches.

When we evangelists come together, we understand each other and we can identify each with the other. That is because, even when we might have different gifts or ways in how we do evangelism, we have more in common than with other types of ministries.

As evangelists we need each other. When we come together to collaborate, we can support each other because we understand the nature of the office of the evangelist.

Sharing the spiritual load

On the road, at the hotel, during the execution of that evangelistic project, we pray for each other, communicate challenges and needs.

One evangelist ministers in one area and another in another area. In our festivals we have evangelists come to specifically minister to single mothers or to people with addictions. That's their gift, and they know how to get into areas where others can not and how to get better results.

We share the load on reaching those people for Christ.

Sharing the emotional load

Evangelizing cities is a huge undertaking.

A city-wide event takes a great deal out of the people responsible for making decisions. It can be tiring. Things can go wrong.

Logistics are not perfect and when we depend on third parties or companies to provide the services needed to make every phase of that event possible, things can go wrong. Someone doesn't show up on time, or someone fails to provide what they were contracted to do.

The stress levels rise, and yes, we trust the Lord to help us confront every situation, but our emotions are affected in the process.

Having a team of people united by one purpose—to bring Christ to that city—is key for the emotional stability of all decision makers. Sometimes a pad on the back or just a simple word of comfort is all that it takes to bring someone under heavy stress back to balance.

We all need to know that we are not alone on this.

Sharing financial responsibility

When organizations get together to reach a city, we can accomplish more financially.

It is expensive to do a city-wide event, a missionary project or a humanitarian mission and sometimes for one ministry alone it is very difficult, but when several ministries come together, they not only share the opportunity of ministering to the needs of the people, they can also share on the financial obligations and that makes the event possible. I will elaborate more on this subject on coming chapters.

In collaboration, everybody wins, everybody benefits, but the kingdom of God benefits more. It is a blessing to see lives transformed by the power of the gospel.

We can do great things in Christ, but the key is to do it together.

CHAPTER 7

50% Of Something Is Better Than 100% Of Nothing

Better to have one handful with quietness than two handfuls with hard work and chasing the wind. Ecclesiastes 4:6 (NLT)

Say you have been called by God to go and reach a city or a specific group of people with the good news.

That is called a vision.

The seed has been planted in your heart, a dream is born. You pray for this. A passion to reach this city or people is growing inside you.

Praise God! That is great, but I have heard many people speak of many visions in the years I have been serving God, and only a few of those visions actually materialized.

Why?

Because a vision without a practical plan to develop it, is only that... *"a vision."*

I believe that if that vision or dream comes from God, He will also give you the strategy to bring it to pass.

So, now you have the vision and you are ready to take action. You are about to go reach that city or people with the message of Christ, and you want to do it alone.

You do the numbers and see how expensive it is to make it happen. Now you might, pray more, try to raise that big budget, and you find out how hard it is to raise money.

At this point you might pray more, wait longer and... well, wait to see if one day, somehow God touches someone to come give you the money.

Some people wait their whole life. Others get discouraged, or surrender to the idea that—oh well—maybe it wasn't God's time or his will.

But wait, His will is that we preach the gospel, so... Is it possible that God has another avenue for you to take?

Yes. There is another avenue.

Let's go back to the vision stage again.

I said before that *"a vision without a practical plan to develop it, is only that... a vision."*

I also said *"I believe if that vision or dream comes from God, He will also give you the strategy to bring it to pass"*, but let me add something else.

That strategy usually involves other people.

It is called "partnership."

You can not reach that city or people alone, but maybe God has placed the same calling in somebody else.

When you collaborate with others, it is easier to accomplish that vision.

You might not be able to raise 100% of that budget, but you might be able to raise 50%.

When you allow others to come in and collaborate with you, you are not only able to raise the budget needed to reach that city or people, you have the opportunity to share ministry with others.

People that have problems with sharing, usually don't accomplish much.

People like that, would rather have 100% of nothing. Yes, the whole vision is yours alone, and you may brag on that, but it's still nothing.

Wouldn't you rather share 50% of it and actually accomplish something.

Yes, it takes generosity, but not really that much, because you are sharing something you never had anyway.

Barnabas and Paul

> *Then Barnabas went on to Tarsus to look for Saul. When he found him, he brought him back to Antioch. Both of them stayed there with the church for a full year, teaching large crowds of people. (It was at Antioch that the believers were first called Christians.) Acts 11:25,26 (NLT)*

If Barnabas had a *lone ranger mentality*[29], he would have probably tried to stay and minister in the city of Antioch by himself.

But Barnabas had a *collaboration mentality.* He knew that Paul had a special gift when it came to preaching.

You can see that demonstrated later when they arrived at Lystra. The Bible says that Paul was *the chief speaker.*

> *When the crowd saw what Paul had done, they shouted in their local dialect, "These men are gods in human form!" They decided that Barnabas was the Greek god Zeus and that Paul was Hermes, since he was the chief speaker. Acts 14:11,12 (NLT)*

You see, Barnabas was a man of great influence[30] and integrity[31]. Plus he was *generous.*

The Bible says that one time, Barnabas *"...sold a field he owned and brought the money to the apostles." Acts 4:37 (NLT)*

64

His generosity is further demonstrated when he shared the door God had opened in Antioch with Paul.

The name Barnabas means *"Son of Encouragement"*, and he honored his name. Paul was a preacher. Here we have a prominent leader[32] and a preacher. What a partnership!

Long term collaboration

When you identify yourself with another evangelist, that relationship can grow and on-going collaboration becomes the solid basis for reaching entire provinces or even countries.

After their work in Antioch, Barnabas and Paul the Apostle undertook missionary journeys together and defended gentile believers against the Judaizers. They traveled together reaching more cities, participated in the *Council of Jerusalem*[33] and successfully evangelized among the *"God-fearing"* gentiles who attended synagogues in various Hellenized cities of Asia Minor[34].

CHAPTER 8

Bad Practices In Collaboration

The festival model I believe God has entrusted us with, is a city-wide type of outreach where many ministries are welcome to come and collaborate.

God has allowed us to combine the humanitarian side of it with different settings, where families can be reached in many different ways, and this goes parallel to the celebration aspect of the event.

In a festival, we usually have tents around the stadium and more than one platform. In those tents, we hold workshops with different themes. While one tent holds workshops for single mothers, another one is bringing workshops for fathers, or mothers, or people with addictions, etc...

We also bring teams of doctors and dentists to minister to the needs of the people of that city.

At the same time there are several other outreaches such as the children's fest, youth tent, and more along those lines while targeting different audiences, groups and generations.

The festivals also have a *Cultural Exchange* time where national and international talents share the platform and a time for proclamation, where the message of Christ is shared from the main platform followed by concerts.

As you can see, in an event with such variety, there are opportunities for many ministries to collaborate. There is everything from childrens' to youth ministries, from drama to mimes, to a full range of presentations and talents.

The ideal

To make this festival a great success it's important that all ministries participating have the same goal in mind—to serve the people of that city. No one looking to advance their own agenda or interests but all working in unity to bring glory to God and reach many with the good news.

Well... What I said in that last paragraph is *"the ideal."*

Sad to say, but in reality we are imperfect people saved by grace and on the road of sanctification, and with our imperfections come many character traits that if not talked about can truly hinder the success of a mission.

I do not desire to abound on the negatives (our kingdom), but before we move on to the positives (His kingdom), I believe it is crucial we deal with areas where we can improve this experience of collaborating for a common cause.

68

Networking as a goal

Probably one of the worst things you can do when you are invited to collaborate at an event, is to use the opportunity primarily to make connections and to try to open doors for yourself.

This shows that you don't care that much for the team work before you but you are more interested in promoting yourself.

Although you will meet other ministries at an event where friendships and new relationships will be born (and that's a good thing), that should not be the goal when you collaborate.

Your goal should be to serve and work toward the common goal of the whole mission. Concentrate on serving.

Allow God to be the one opening doors for you and not you on your own strength.

> *I know all the things you do, and I have opened a door for you that no one can close...*
> *Revelation 3:8 (NLT)*

Booking instead of serving

I have seen this more than once. An evangelist or an artist that we invited to serve in a city with us, and when we left the city he or she already had booked several engagements to go back to that city on their own a month later.

It would not be a problem if the pastors of that city invite you because they were blessed when they saw you minister and they want to have you back. That would be a blessing.

The problem is when you—instead of serving the people of that city—used your time for networking and offering your services.

Liabilities

I remember one time I invited a family of artists to serve at a festival. Our organization covered all of their expenses, including air travel, accommodations and honoraries.

After the festival ended, they stayed in the city for a month.

It is interesting that about two weeks after the festival, we started receiving at our office some complaints from pastors of that city.

The pastors complained of some of the practices this family of artists had when it came to asking for money and charging for their services.

They knew that we don't endorse those practices. They knew we don't collect offerings at our events. Actually, we don't mention money at all when we do a city-wide event. Everything at a festival is free—even concerts.

Still, the pastors associated them with us, because we worked together (we were the ones bringing them to that city at first), and the pastors were confused. These people used our name and the contacts they gained at the event. They took advantage of the trust we had built with the pastors of that city.

Other Bad Practices

Self promotion

A collaboration event is not an opportunity for you and your gift to shine. It really hurts teamwork and the mission when one person is seeking to be noticed above the rest. Be wise when you are handed the microphone. Remember that Christ is the one taking the entire honor and all the glory. The event is not about you and/or your great name. It is about Christ and His message.

A ministry has invited you to minister to their audience. Be at a church, a platform in the festival or in a tent ministering to a small group inside the stadium.

Do not constantly talk about yourself, your ministry, your accomplishments, or how well known you are. Besides not being a blessing, you are taking advantage of the trust you have been given to promote your agenda. This is not honest and it's a bad practice when you are invited anywhere.

> Let someone else praise you, not your own mouth—a stranger, not your own lips.
> Proverbs 27:2 (NLT)

Collaboration is about *team work*. It's not a cliché, it's a practical reality.

You must think about the well-being of others in the team. It's not about one name, one person, or who goes first or last to the platform. It's about getting the work done.

It takes many to raise a harvest.

Photo opportunities

Yes. It is important that when you are invited to collaborate in a project you create a record, a journal, and/or perhaps a report. You would want to show your donors (the people that helped you to get to that event), what you did and how your ministry within the festival was a blessing to the people you ministered to. That is all perfectly fine and recommended.

What it's not a good idea is to use the event as a photo opportunity to build a reputation out of proportion.

You might have the opportunity to be on the main platform to share a testimony or a few words and/or to salute the audience. It's not wise that you post or print (on social networks, blogs or newsletters) a picture of you on the main platform (without explaining your role within the event) giving the impression that you held "a massive event" on your own. This is not only a bad practice, it is also dishonest and it will only hurt your ministry. Plus, you might lose the trust of the organization inviting you to collaborate.

Copyright violations

The use of materials that are intellectual property is an

area where you want to pay attention. Do not use the name, logo, festival art or materials of the inviting organization (without their permission) to give the impression that you are being endorsed.

If you are seeking the endorsement of a leader you respect, do it the proper way and in writing.

Lessons learned

There are a few principles I've learned related to bad collaboration experiences.

Lesson 1: **Those who would abuse your trust for their own benefit can do it well, but only one time.**

You can read in the book of second Kings, of how Gehazi took advantage of the access he had to his master's friend. Yes, he was able to gain something, but could only do it one time.

> *But Elisha asked him, "Don't you realize that I was there in spirit when Naaman stepped down from his chariot to meet you? Is this the time to receive money and clothing, olive groves and vineyards, sheep and cattle, and male and female servants? Because you have done this, you and your descendants will suffer from Naaman's leprosy forever." When Gehazi left the room, he was covered with leprosy; his skin was white as snow. 2 Kings 5:26,27 (NLT)*

Lesson 2: **Loyalty is determined by the use of trust.**

We have to take chances. Especially with people we collaborate with for the first time, when we bring someone on board, and have to trust to them part of the work.

Only when you see what they do with the trust you gave them, can you trust them again and with more.

In time, with those who value that trust and demonstrate loyalty, transparency, faithfulness, you will establish an on-going, long-term, working relationship.

Those long-term friends become more like family members.

A wise man once told me *"you cannot trust a person who only has new friends."*

A person that only looks to benefit from other people, usually ends up alone.

Can you imagine how much Paul trusted Timothy, that he would send him to a city knowing that his spiritual son would represent him well—and not only that, but also represented the message very effectively.

> *That's why I have sent Timothy, my beloved and faithful child in the Lord. He will remind you of how I follow Christ Jesus, just as I teach in all the churches... 1 Corinthians 4:17 (NLT)*

Lesson 3: **Trust again.**

Yes. There are people that will try to partner with you for the wrong reasons, but there are many that are truly seeking to please God, and serve HIS kingdom.

Do not allow the bad experiences you had with some, prevent you from trusting others.

Many will show good intentions, and the fruits of their collaboration will surpass the negatives by a long way.

I'm a believer on the benefits of collaboration. Our ministry is a living proof of that.

When we do a mass event, hundreds come to work on the team (not only ministers and artists). At every city-wide event, we rely on hundreds of volunteers including all the professionals that come to serve in each humanitarian mission.

The vast majority comes to serve... to serve God and to serve others. That is the spirit of the event and the negatives are very small in comparison to the results of every event.

Most people involved are working to build HIS kingdom and to bring honor and glory to HIM: The King of kings and Lord of lords.

CHAPTER 9

It's All About Jesus

Pray ye therefore the Lord of the harvest, that he will send forth labourers into his harvest.
Matthew 9:38 (KJV)

He is The Lord of the harvest. It is all about Jesus.

For collaboration to be effective; when we come together we must put aside our interests and agendas, and unite—keeping in mind that it's all about HIM.

If you put HIM first, and become part of the team without looking for recognition—but serving and putting others before you—God will use you. You will be an instrument of great blessing to many.

Also keep in mind that it's not your gift what brings people to Christ. It is the work of the Holy Spirit. So, when we join the Holy Spirit in what HE is doing, we become part of HIS work.

The one who regulates the harvest and effectively calls people to salvation, is the Lord. He is the Lord of the Harvest.

It's for HIS church

You cannot reach a city without partnering with the local churches. In most cities, when we finish an event, we send all the collaborating evangelists to the churches on Sunday. The idea is to re-enforce the follow-up work, and to bless the nationals.

We establish relations with those churches months before the event and they are an integral part of the follow-up work for months after the event.

It is important that when you—as part of a collaborative event—are sent to a local church, keep in mind that your message and ministry is part of a greater plan for the city.

You must work on adding value to what happened at the festival and communicating to the nationals the responsibility of caring for the harvest.

That's why it is so important that all evangelists collaborating on an event, meet and review the goals for reaching the city and the plan for what happens in that city after the event.

Even if you are invited back by one of the churches, you must keep in mind what brought you to that city in the first place. It is important to keep representing the original project because the nationals will always link you with the ministry that brought you to them. What a responsibility!

CHAPTER 10

Good Practices In Collaboration

I always say that *"if we eat together, we can work together."*

It is incredible how many things Jesus accomplished when seating with others at a table. I believe that some of his greater messages were delivered around a meal.

I've learned that when I go to a city, I must eat with the pastors. I try to have breakfast or lunch with them, either on a large scale, or on a small group—sometimes with two or three pastors. We eat together, we spend time together. I listen to their vision for the city. I listen to what they have to say about the work of God in that city, about their ministries, their dreams, their struggles. I listen and I listen.

We must level with the nationals

Level with the Nationals. Lower your profile... and you shall conquer the city for Christ.

The day of the star evangelist is over. The man hiding in a cave (or hotel room) and just coming out to preach *"under the spotlight"* does not help the missions work. That type of attitude creates distance between you (the evangelist) and the nationals.

If you cannot seat where they sit, you have no right to tell them what's good for them.

Many years ago, when I was a young missionary, God opened doors for me to preach to several indigenous groups in Mexico.

There were four main language groups we were targeting: Mixteco Alto, Mixteco Bajo, Zapoteco and Triqui.

When they came under the tent, I had to use four translators. A ten minute message would become a forty minute message. That was fun, but I also learned how important it is for their culture that you eat with them.

I became their friend. There were missions where I had to sleep in a hammock, walk around barefoot, and listen to their tales and stories and complaints.

God allowed us to lead many indigenous people to Christ in a period of a few years.

God will use you in the nations of the world, but you have to level with people, and when you become part of a collaborative event, you need to level with the nationals before you can be respected and trusted by them.

Then, you'll be able to reach their people with the message of the gospel.

I'm writing this book right after we've completed a festival project in the city of Turrialba, Costa Rica. It was a good experience.

At the closing of the event, we knew for sure, God had touched the city. At every event, we get to see great joy and good testimonies from the people of that city, but this one was different. Something happened in the life of the pastors of Turrialba.

After all had concluded at the stadium on the last night of the event, as we were getting ready to leave the place to go back to the hotel, a pastor's wife came to my wife and I with tears of joy in her eyes and she said: *"The thing that has impacted my husband and all the other pastors the most is that the evangelists that came did not come as celebrities. They are 'down to earth' people that were willing to put on their t-shirts like any other volunteer and mingle with the people and serve them... We have never seen something like that in ministers and I think that is what inspired the pastors to roll up their sleeves and work together for the first time in this city."*

The city mayor[35] said this about the event:

> *"This event has shown us that as a community, we can come together and do great things for the people of the city. We have never seen such unity*

like this before, there is joy and people want to work together. Thank you for coming to serve, asking for nothing in return."

More testimonies like that came that night, and they are still coming. There is great joy in the city and the impact is being extended as the pastors *"in unity"* are following the program that will integrate the new believers to the churches.

For twelve weeks following the event, these leaders are having home studies with our discipleship program[36]. They are serving the new believers by identifying their immediate needs (counseling, jobs, etc...) and helping, and providing transportation to bring them to church on Sunday.

Good things are happening in that city as I write these lines, but that is not the work of one man. It is impossible to touch a city in so many areas with the gifts of one evangelist or one organization alone. It's the result of a collaborative effort, and it all started with coming to the city and leveling with the pastors while serving the nationals.

> *But among you it will be different. Whoever wants to be a leader among you must be your servant... Matthew 20:26 (NLT)*

Other Good Practices

Look at the clock

If the platform manager or program director says 15 minutes, it is 15 minutes. If he/she says one song, it is one song.

When you take more time than you are given, you affect the rest of the program.

I've heard people say: *"I got inspired by the Holy Ghost and could not stop"* or things like that.

The truth is that when you have no respect for the time you are given, you are also disrespecting your fellow evangelist or singer who is coming after you.

Being considerate with others is a blessing and keeps the event flowing.

Respect the structure

Luis Palau says: *"Our message is sacred, but the method is not[37]."*

God gives different gifts and inspires different models and ways of reaching the lost to every evangelist.

Your gift is unique and your model very effective, but when you are a visiting evangelist assisting or collaborating with another ministry, it is important that you respect their model and ways of doing things.

The minute you try to change things using an excuse such as, *I know a better way,* you not only disrupt the flow of the event, you create disunity.

83

As evangelists we need to learn to trust what God has given to other evangelists.

You will be more of a blessing if you submit to what's already established than to try to change it.

My grandma used to say: *"when you are visiting another house, don't take your shoes off."*

You should respect the rules, especially when you are in a foreign country. The way you behave at the hotel, at the airport, or at the event's venue is extremely important. Respect the organizations that are working with the hosting ministry.

Read the instructions

When we launch a missions' project or festival and welcome other evangelists or mission workers to collaborate, we publish a brochure with all the information about the project. That includes, information about the city, the culture, the dates, traveling details, schedules, etc...

I believe other ministries organizing similar type of outreaches do the same.

When someone is interested in being a part of that mission, we send them the brochure and direct them to the event's website for more information. Also, if people have questions, we gladly respond via e-mail.

Nevertheless. We receive an incredible number of e-mails from people asking questions like: *"What are the dates?"* or *"What is the name of the city?"* which clearly tells us, people are not reading the brochures.

As I said, we gladly respond to these questions, not a big deal when we are talking pre-event.

The problem is when you arrive at that country without reading the information. You are risking arriving and no one waiting to pick you up, or landing at the wrong airport. We have seen that happen.

It is also important that you read the instructions, so you know at what time to wake up, have breakfast, go to prayer, and be ready to get on the bus to go to the venue.

You need to know what's the schedule. At what time you are ministering. What message to prepare, etc...

It is important that we read the instructions and all information regarding the project.

Be flexible

In the past, when going to a mission abroad, I have given every member of the team a rubber band to wear on their wrist. I tell them: *"Remember: 'Elasticity will help you stay calm in the middle of ever changing situations.'"*

You see. We organize an event. We hire different services

from different companies or partner with other organizations to do something.

Sometimes (particularly in our loved Latin America) things don't go according to plan.

The bus driver was stuck in traffic and could not be on time at the airport.

Something burned and the food could not be ready on time. Flight got cancelled and you arrived a day later.

There is a number of possible things that could go wrong.

You need to be flexible to be a team player. If you get all stressed out and lose your patience, the way you react to things can affect someone else in the team.

The other things are human mistakes.

Someone in the team will make a mistake. Forget something. Break something. Accidents happen. It is the nature of our humanity.

It is important that you allow room for others to make mistakes. Be graceful to others in the team.

Remember that we all make mistakes and when you make yours, you would like the same grace to be extended to you.

So... be flexible. God has it all under control.

Be financially responsible

When you decide to be part of a mission, there are expenses involved (hotel, transportation, food, etc.) and in some cases you might agree to raise funds to share part of the event expenses.

There are many types of collaboration models and opportunities.

Sometimes, two evangelists get together to reach a city and they agree to each cover 50% of the event expenses.

Whatever the arrangement is, it is very important that you cover your responsibilities and on time.

Many times organizing committees have to pay for half of the contracts ahead of time.

A city-wide event will create many expenses months before the actual event.

Keeping your financial commitments speaks highly of you and keeps the doors open.

Back home we have a saying that goes something like this: *"Clear numbers, long friendships."* Probably a North American version would be: *"Good fences make good neighbors."*

People will provide good references when you are responsible with your financial commitments.

Choose a good reputation over great riches; being held in high esteem is better than silver or gold.
Proverbs 22:1 (NLT)

Good testimony

Show a good testimony, because everything you do, (good or bad) reflects on the name and the work of the organization responsible for the event. Actually, that is one of the main prayer concerns we share with our partners—that we may leave a good report in the city where we are serving.

The nationals are looking at you—that is, all the team of volunteers and people serving alongside the evangelists.

As a man or a woman of God, it is necessary you show good character at all times.

Pray that God will give you patience and show your love for the people you are reaching.

They will pay more attention at what you do off the platform than what you say when you are preaching.

The nationals are looking at you when you are at the hotel, on the bus, at the table eating and when you are making quick decisions. They also pay attention to your jokes.

The pastors are also looking at you. Remember that some pastors are skeptical of the office of the evangelist due to all the abuses they have seen in the name of evangelism.

I believe that restoring the trust in the office of the evangelist is also one of our goals when we come to do an evangelistic event in the mission field.

CHAPTER 11

International Collaboration

Wandering Missionaries

In the Didache[38], Apostles are called *"wandering missionaries"* when referring to their moving from place to place ministry.

As evangelists we are called to go. We are always on the move. From city to city, from nation to nation, we are always taking the good news to the end of the earth.

As we go to new cities, I find that more people—even from third-world countries—are called to go.

The idea that missionaries are only from the U.S., is an old idea.

The mentality of being on the receiving end is changing for many in the nations. God is calling a new generation of traveling missionaries—from other countries—that are leaving their hometowns and going to the ends of the earth.

What does that mean for collaboration?

It means we are forming more and more, international teams

to reach cities.

Allow me to give you an example.

In our last festival in Costa Rica[39], we needed a team of about six hundred people. Many of them were being mobilized to work as volunteers, counselors, etc... and that team is usually composed of locals. So, I'm only going to count those who came to participate in active ministry.

We only had twelve evangelists coming from the U.S. including myself, plus our team from San Diego (about thirty in total).

It is impossible to cover the whole ministry at the festival with thirty people. We needed people to serve in the children's ministry—that is, a tent (all day long) during two days plus the children's fest. Only for the children's ministry we needed those who use drama, those who use arts, mimes, musicians and many other types of creative ministries to effectively communicate the message of Christ to that generation.

Well, we had several ministers specialized in child evangelism come from other cities.

And we had others travel from other countries in Latin America, some from Venezuela, others from Guatemala, México, etc...

The same happened for the youth ministries, and for the extreme sports section of the festival.

Our team from the U.S. trained about seven hundred in the *School of Creative Evangelism*™, and three hundred of them became mentors to do the follow-up for twelve weeks after the festival (they are the ones integrating the new believers to the churches).

The work of evangelism in the nations takes well organized teams of ministers specialized in the different areas of need, found in a society full of problems.

I'm finding—as I move from place to place—that God is calling people from different cultures and backgrounds to form those teams.

This is true collaboration—international collaboration.

CHAPTER 12

Who Is Your Mentor?

Listen to advice

Collaboration is an old art. It's been around for a long time.

I think it's important for young evangelists to listen to advice and learn from the others that have done it before them.

I've been greatly influenced by what I call elders in the faith.

Cesar Vicente was a baptist preacher. At one point he was the superintendent of a whole district at Northeastern United States.

He gave me exceptional good advice in several areas of ministry when I was starting up as a young itinerant evangelist in the early eighties, but probably the most valuable advice he ever gave me was when I went to him one day and told him I wanted to write a book.

His immediate answer was:

—You are not ready... wait twenty five years.

At the time I did not understand, but I respected him as

a man of God, so I listened to his advice, and I waited, and waited, and waited... and twenty five years went by.

I'm so glad I listened to him. If I had written a book then I'm sure I would have regretted it. Doctrinally, I was still being formed. There were many things I had to go through. I needed maturity.

Twenty five years later, I started to write.

I have much to learn still, but today I'm much more careful when choosing words, when ordering the flow of ideas, and making sure the books are written with the right purpose— that is—to minister to others without looking for recognition or status.

I still make mistakes when I write, but God has been gracious surrounding me with wise people—way smarter than me.

I also seek the advice of older authors, mentors and elders. Their opinions matter, and I don't think I could accomplish anything without having them in my life.

Old Evangelists know better

I love to seat and listen to my mentors. Those who have ran the race and have been around longer than me.

Sometimes I take a plane just to go spend one day at a closed meeting or training session with one of these old-timers I truly respect. I always learn something new. Some of these mentors have been in the ministry—specifically in missions and evangelism—for fifty or sixty years.

Every time I do this, I see how much I still need to learn.

Who is your mentor?

Who is that person you respect and admire.

Yes, I said "admire."

You learn not only from people you respect, but from those you *"admire."*

Admiration produces inspiration.

Who inspires you?

That brother or sister that has been around awhile—that has traveled the road you are in right now.

I'm not talking about someone with *"star status."* Being a well known artist or personality in the christian scene does not necessarily qualifies someone as a mentor.

Collaboration is a mentoring opportunity

When you travel to be part of an event or project to serve in whatever area you are designated to, there is a good opportunity to learn.

Pay attention to the leader or leaders of the organization

97

responsible for the event.

Good Mentor Bad Mentor

An example of a good mentor is Paul.

His relation with those collaborating with him in the ministry is a fatherly relationship.

That is the case with Timothy.

> *That's why I have sent Timothy, my beloved and faithful child in the Lord. He will remind you of how I follow Christ Jesus, just as I teach in all the churches wherever I go. 1 Cor 4:17 (NLT)*

The same with Titus.

> *I am writing to Titus, my true son in the faith that we share... Titus 1:4 (NLT)*

Paul guided and prepared them in a way that they could represent him well.

Paul is confident that when Timothy went to the Corinthians, he was going to speak just as if he was there, *"just as I teach in all the churches"* Paul said.

So, a good mentor will prepare you and send you—being proud of you at the same time.

An example of a bad mentor is King Saul.

98

David always looked up to him as a father figure, but Saul, instead of being proud of David's victories, became jealous.

> *When the victorious Israelite army was returning home after David had killed the Philistine, women from all the towns of Israel came out to meet King Saul. They sang and danced for joy with tambourines and cymbals. This was their song: "Saul has killed his thousands, and David his ten thousands!" This made Saul very angry. "What's this?" he said. "They credit David with ten thousands and me with only thousands. Next they'll be making him their king!"*
> *1 Samuel 18:6-8 (NLT)*

You cannot have an insecure mentor.

An insecure leader instead of empowering you for the future, will hurt you with words and actions. He will always try to have all the attention for himself and will not allow anybody to get credit for their efforts.

Remember, mentoring is motivated by love, and in collaboration the older must be generous for this type of relationship to work.

Author's Note:

(Before you read the next chapter)

If you are a millennial reading this book, I understand that the fact that I'm categorizing your generation as a group, might be offensive and interpreted as stereotyping. I assure you that it is not my intention to be critical or disrespectful of your generation by using apparent generalizations.

The characteristics noted here are for the purpose of making the sharing of the *Good News* relevant to the smarter and most informed generation that has ever existed.

CHAPTER 13

Reaching The Millennials

The *"One Man of God[40]"* ministry concept is not attractive to the millennials.

This generation, besides not being too trusting of personalities or charismatic leaders—and with justifiable reasons—are more oriented towards the group / community concept.

Millennials are team-oriented, according to Neil Howe[41], an authority on generations. Their desire for community is deep.

Because of these characteristics, an outreach done by a group, ministering to a group is a lot more attractive than the idea of the *"One Man of God"* figure.

What to keep in mind when trying to reach Millennials

1- Be fast

For millennials, there's nothing worth saying that can't be said in 140 characters or less. It's not that they can't handle long-form pitches, they just know you can do better. So do better. Like I have said before, *"the days of long sermonizing messages are gone."*

When we do festivals abroad (and I will talk about Millennials affecting people groups in other countries), we keep this principle in mind to the point that we keep all proclamation messages to 10 minutes or less.

2- Be transparent

Millennials may come across as arrogant and entitled, but they're not stupid, and they know when you are trying to sell them an idea. So rather than trying to conspicuously entice them with deep theological reasonings, be real and let them see how imperfect you are and why you still need help like anyone else. They'll appreciate the honesty.

3- Don't "technologize" your language to level with them

By their own definition, Millennials are in part defined by their use of and reliance on technology. But you should resist the urge to attempt to "speak their language"—Millennials can smell your "pretending" a mile away. Remember, Millennials are digital natives—they don't use technology; they live it, and they do so subconsciously[42].

CHAPTER 14

The Nets Are Tearing

When he had finished speaking, he said to Simon, "Now go out where it is deeper, and let down your nets to catch some fish." "Master," Simon replied, "we worked hard all last night and didn't catch a thing. But if you say so, I'll let the nets down again." And this time their nets were so full of fish they began to tear! A shout for help brought their partners in the other boat, and soon both boats were filled with fish and on the verge of sinking. Luke 5:4-7 (NLT)

When there is abundance of fish, we need help to pull the nets.

City-wide events are like a big fishing adventure. When we let down those nets, they come back full of fish and to pull out those heavy nets we will need help.

That's when collaboration comes in.

In the story I quoted above, the Bible says that when they saw that the nets started to tear, *"a shout for help brought their partners in the other boat."*

That's it. *"A shout for help"* is needed to bring the *"partners"* in.

That's exactly what happens when we announce an opportunity to collaborate in the mission field. We are bringing in partners to help us pull the nets out of the water.

When we all see those nets full of fish, we rejoice. As evangelists we are fulfilling the call of being *"fishers of men."*

> *And he saith unto them, Follow me, and I will make you fishers of men. Matthew 4:19 (KJV)*

Most of the problems between churches and pastors in a city can be fixed with a harvest.

As collaborators, we not only help to bring new believers into the churches. Our work has great influence in the health of the local congregations.

In any city, there are always conflicts between pastors. Sad to say, but it's the truth.

One pastor is not that happy that one of his members left the congregation and went to another pastor's church.

By the way, when there is no fishing (evangelism) in a city, you see a lot of rotation.

You might see a new church growing really fast, but it's not actually new believers coming in.

It's the people that rotate from church to church. Some attracted to every new thing or wave, others that have been hurt and need help or were lacking good teaching and a move was necessary and well justified.

Whatever the reason. It is more common to see rotation in a city where there is no healthy evangelism.

But... when there is a net full of fish, I have seen those problems go away.

Pastors are busy working together to pull that heavy net out of the water, and they have no time for differences.

Unity among pastors is one of the blessings a mass event brings to a city.

Collaboration is important.

It's the way fishers of men can work together to impact cities and provinces and even whole nations.

I have seen it, time and time again.

We need to work together to bring the good news to every new generation. Together we can.

Notes:

Part I

1- Rechtgläubigkeit und Ketzerei im ältesten Christentum, published in 1934. The English translation, entitled Orthodoxy and Heresy in Earliest Christianity, published in 1971. It was translated by the Philadelphia Seminar on Christians Origins, edited by Robert Kraft and Gerhard Krodel, and published by Fortress. The original German edition was published by J. C. B. Mohr (Paul Siebeck) in Tübingen.

2- Barrack Obama said in a June 2007 speech, "Whatever we once were, we are no longer a Christian nation; at least not just. We are also a Jewish nation, a Muslim nation, and a Buddhist nation, and Hindu nation, and a nation of nonbelievers." Obama, Barack. " 'Call to Renewal' Keynote Address." Obama.senate.gov. Washington, D.C., 28 June 2006.

3- Founded 1974. http://www.lausanne.org/en/ (Accessed June 24, 2014) Initially as the Lausanne Continuation Committee following the International Congress on World Evangelization; in 1976 the Lausanne Committee for World Evangelization was established. Records of the Lausanne Committee for World Evangelization http://www2.wheaton.edu/bgc/archives/GUIDES/046.htm (Accessed June 24, 2014).

4- 1982 Lausanne Committee Chicago meeting and Joshua Project.

5- A people group is considered unreached (UPG) when there is no indigenous community of believing Christians able to engage this people group with church planting. Technically speaking, the percentage of evangelical Christians in this people group is less than 2 percent. People Groups http://www.peoplegroups.org/ (Accessed June 24, 2014).

6- It is important to note that this does not mean every individual within an unreached people group has never heard of Jesus or understood the message of salvation. There is often a small percentage (less than 2%) Christ-followers in these groups, but the vast majority of the group has minimal, if any, exposure to the person of Jesus Christ and the Good News of God's free gift of salvation. For arguments sake, suppose for every true believer there are ten who have heard of Jesus but not embraced Him. That would mean that in an unreached people group 20% had heard of Jesus and 80% had not. In other words, possibly 4 out of 5 individuals in an unreached people group are totally unaware of the Messiah.

7- What is the 10/40 Window? Copyright © 2014 Joshua Project. A ministry of the U.S. Center for World Mission. http://joshuaproject. net/resources/articles/10_40_window (Accessed June 24, 2014).

8- North America and the Caribbean http://www.ethne.net/prayer/ regions/prayer-for-the-north-america-caribbean-region (Accessed June 24, 2014).

9- Central and South America http://www.ethne.net/prayer/ regions/prayer-for-the-central-south-america-region (Accessed June 24, 2014).

10- Millennials are now the largest generational demographic, subsuming the place of priority long held by the Baby Boomers. http://www.travelpulse.com/news/travel-agents/how-do-you-market-to-millennials-authenticity-experience-and-free-wi-fi.html (Accessed June 24, 2014).

11- Generations: The History of America's Future, 1584 to 2069 [Paperback] Quill; Reprint edition (September 30, 1992) ISBN 978-0688119126.

12- Marketing to Leading-Edge Baby Boomers: Perceptions, Principles, Practices & Predictions Paperback, Paramount Market Publishing, Inc. (March 10, 2006) ISBN 978-0976697350.

13- How Do You Market to Millennials? Authenticity, Experience and Free Wi-Fi by David Cogswell http://www.travelpulse.com/news/travel-agents/how-do-you-market-to-millennials-authenticity-experience-and-free-wi-fi.html (Accessed June 24, 2014).

14- Study Finds Millennial Generation's Power to Influence Is Increasing. http://www.edelman.com/news/study-finds-millennial-generations-power-to-influence-is-increasing/ (Accessed June 24, 2014).

15- Michele Serro, a former associate partner at IDEO, a leading design and innovation consulting firm, and founder of New York City-based Doorsteps, an online tool for prospective homeowners that targets young buyers.

Part II

16- Dr. John Haggai http://www.haggai-institute.com/who-we-are/how-we-began/ (accessed on June 11, 2014).

17- The legitimacy of colonialism has been a longstanding concern for political and moral philosophers in the Western tradition. At least since the Crusades and the conquest of the Americas, political theorists have struggled with the difficulty of reconciling ideas about justice and natural law with the practice of European sovereignty over non-Western peoples. First published Tue May 9, 2006; substantive revision Tue Apr 10, 2012 © Stanford University http://plato.stanford.edu/entries/colonialism/ (accessed on June 11, 2014).

18- Recent Pentecostal Scandals, First published July 18, 2006 by David Cloud, Fundamental Baptist Information Service, P.O. Box 610368, Port Huron, MI 48061 http://www.wayoflife.org/database/recent_pentecostal_scandals.html (accessed on June 11, 2014).

19- Nicholas A. Christakis, MD, PhD, is a professor at *Harvard University* with joint appointments in the Departments of Health Care Policy, Sociology, and Medicine, and in 2009 was named one of

Time magazine's 100 most influential people in the world.

20- *Connected: The Surprising Power of Our Social Networks and How They Shape Our Lives—How Your Friends' Friends' Friends Affect* [Paperback] ISBN 978-0316036139 Authors: Nicholas A. Christakis, MD, PhD and James H. Fowler, PhD, an associate professor at the *University of California*, San Diego, in the Department of Political Science and The Center for Wireless and Population Health Systems, and was named one of the "most inspiring scientists" by the San Diego Science Festival.

21- "Take less space." This phrase was taken from a message by Wendy Palau during the *Re:Fuel Conference 2014* at the *Luis Palau Association* headquarters. Although the message was delivered in another context, the author saw how the principles in the message directly apply to collaboration.

22- Generosity. http://en.wikipedia.org/wiki/Generosity (Accessed April 22, 2014).

23- Merriam-Webster (An Encyclopædia Britannica Company) http://www.merriam-webster.com/dictionary/generosity (Accessed April 20, 2014).

24- *What is Generosity? The Science of Generosity.* A research University of Notre Dame. The Science of Generosity Usage http://generosityresearch.nd.edu/more-about-the-initiative/what-is-generosity/ (Accessed May 2, 2014).

25- A mantle is a loose-fitting cloak worn over the shoulders. "Picking up the mantle" expresses a concept similar to "passing the torch." The key difference is the timing of the transfer of authority. In the first expression, the leader departs and leaves behind his mantle for someone to assume; in the second, the leader hands off his role to someone else, then departs. The expression comes from the Bible. In 2 Kings, Chapter 2, Verses 1-15, the prophet Elijah is carried up to heaven by a whirlwind. He leaves behind his mantle, and his disciple, Elisha, picks it up. Reference: http://www.ehow. com/facts_5977599_meaning-picking-up-mantle_.html (Accessed May 1, 2014).

26- *What Are The Core Principles of Collaboration?* Adi Gaskell January 3, 2012 Social Business News http://www.socialbusinessnews. com/what-are-the-core-principles-of-collaboration/ (Accessed April 18, 2014).

27- *The Wisdom of Crowds* ISBN 978-0385721707 In this book, author, James Surowiecki explores a deceptively simple idea: Large groups of people are smarter than an elite few, no matter how brilliant–better at solving problems, fostering innovation, coming to wise decisions, even predicting the future.

28- The *Luis Palau NGA* serves member evangelists through mentoring and equipping, collaborative outreach events, and training and conferences. More information at http://www.palau. org/alliance (Accessed April 14, 2014).

29- Lone ranger mentality. Lone Ranger, hero of an American radio and television western. First Known Use: 1969 / One who acts alone and without consultation or the approval of others; broadly: loner. Source: Merriam-Webster (An Encyclopædia Britannica Company).

30- Barnabas, born Joseph, was an early Christian, one of the earliest Christian disciples in Jerusalem. "Barnabas." Cross, F. L., ed. The Oxford dictionary of the Christian church. New York: Oxford University Press 2005.

31- Acts presents the evangelizing apostle and church leader Barnabas as a model of integrity and character. Calling him a good man (Acts 11:24), a prophet and teacher (13:1), an apostle (14:14) and one through whom God worked miracles (15:12), Acts loads him with accolades. Acts recounts the times he faced persecution (13:45; 14:19) and risked his life for the name of the Lord Jesus Christ (15:26). http://www.biblicalarchaeology.org/daily/people-cultures-in-the-bible/people-in-the-bible/barnabas-an-encouraging-early-church-leader/ (Accessed April 18, 2014).

32- Harris names him as a "prominent leader" of the early church in Jerusalem. Harris, Stephen L., *Understanding the Bible. Palo Alto: Mayfield.* 1985. (Accessed April 18, 2014).

33- Durant, Will. *Caesar and Christ.* New York: Simon and Schuster 1972. They traveled together reaching more cities (c 45-47) and participated in the Council of Jerusalem (c 50).

34- Harris, Stephen L., *Understanding the Bible.* Palo Alto: Mayfield. 1985.

35- Lic. Maria Elena Montoya Piedra, Mayor of Turrialba. Started governing in February 11, 2011. Source: http://es.wikipedia.org/wiki/Cant%C3%B3n_de_Turrialba (Accessed April 3, 2014) Turrialba is the name of the fifth canton in the province of Cartago in Costa Rica. Source: http://en.wikipedia.org/wiki/Turrialba_%28canton%29 (Accessed April 3, 2014).

36- *Transformación de Ciudad™ Discípulo 3.0* is the discipleship / follow-up material that was distributed to the leaders that came to the SCE *(School of Creative Evangelism™)* to be trained.

37- *By All Means* by Luis Palau March 29, 1012 Source: http://blogs.palau.org/archives/by-all-means (Accessed April 15, 2014).

38- Draper, J. A. (2006). *"The Apostolic Fathers: The Didache."* The Expository Times 117 (5): 177–81.

39- At the moment when this section of the book was written (April / May 2014).

40- The "One Man of God" syndrome. Steve Hill, *End the Celebrity Syndrome in the Church.* http://www.charismanews.com/opinion/from-the-frontlines/39925-steve-hill-end-the-celebrity-syndrome-in-the-church (Accessed March 17, 2015).

41- Neil Howe is an American historian, economist, and demographer. He is best known for his work with William Strauss on social generations and generational cycles in American history. http://www.lifecourse.com/about/leadership-team/howe.html (Accessed February 27, 2015).

42- Thomas Pardee, *Media-Savvy Gen Y Finds Smart and Funny Is 'New Rock 'n' Roll'. Transparency, Authenticity and Relevance Key When Marketing to These Quiet Agents of Change.* Published on October 11, 2010. http://adage.com/article/news/marketing-media-savvy-gen-y-transparency-authenticity/146388/ (Accessed June 24, 2014).

Together we can reach more...
Collaborative projects of the *JA Pérez Association*
in Latin America.

For we are labourers together with God: ye are God's husbandry, ye are God's building. *1 Corinthians 3:9 (KJV)*

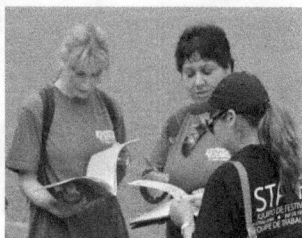

It takes a team to raise a harvest!
The preparations for a city-wide event can take months. The actual week of the event, the team arrives to work with the nationals on training and preparing the churches for the impact, also on the logistics surrounding the venue.

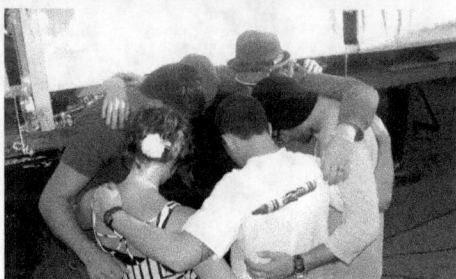

Loving the city

Before the festival starts, team members visit schools, orphanages, and impoverished areas where humanitarian missions take place. We also send street evangelism teams (led by our partner evangelists) to every corner of the city.

118

Equipping the nationals

For four weeks (before the event) the *School of Creative Evangelism*™ takes place. We train the nationals with the *City Transformation*™ materials to do the 12 weeks discipleship and follow up program. Besides creating a culture of personal evangelism in the city, they learn how to care for the new believers, integrating them to the local churches. Our partner evangelists also deliver conferences for the family, and for pastors and leaders.

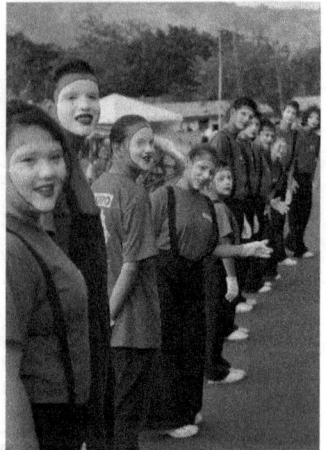

Cultural Exchange™

At the festival, the *Cultural Exchange*™ will unite national and international talents on the platform with music, drama, folkloric dances and many other forms of art.

Children's Ministries

Clowns, mimes, dances, and many other creative ways of presenting the good news to children are used by many of the team members coming from other countries to partner with us on the event. We also have the *Children's Fest* on the main platform each day of the event.

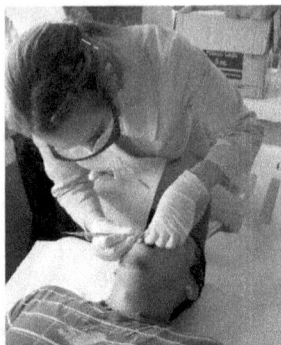

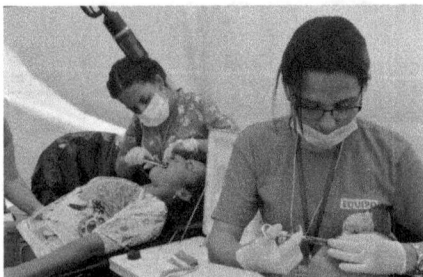

Service

At every event we partner with Medical Doctors, Dentists and Counselors that come to serve the people of that city. During the day—at the stadium—doctors and counselors assist families in need. Not only with medicine and humanitarian aid. Their spiritual needs are also ministered to. Many come to Christ during the day, which becomes part of the great harvest in the event in general. Demonstrating the love of Christ through practical service is a key element of every city outreach.

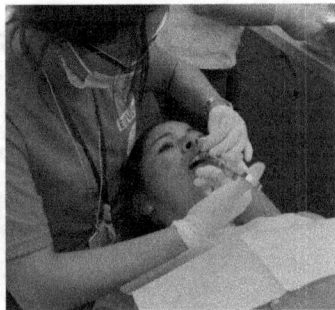

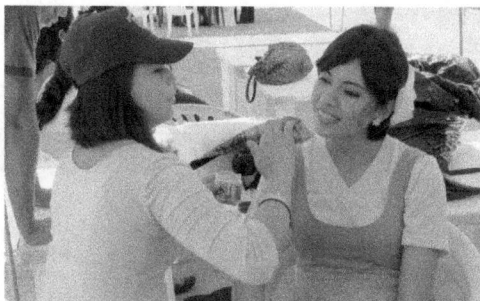

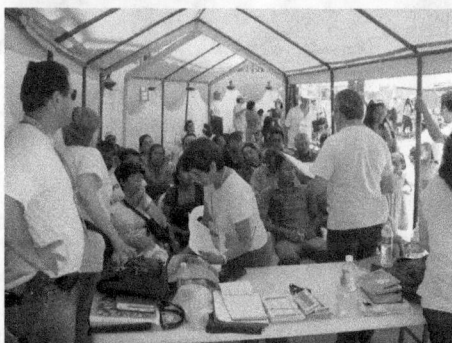

Specific Ministries

Tents with workshops for families, youth, single mothers, battered women, addictions, etc... operate throughout the day around the stadium. Christ is also presented and many are reached this way. We aim to target all audiences and generations by interest and age.

Proclamation

I'm blessed to be able to share the platform with world evangelists I love and respect. I also take mentoring very seriously. Bringing on the platform younger evangelists has become part of the process of empowering them to do mass evangelism.

The Harvest

When a city or province is impacted, often government leaders—such as Mayors and Congressmen—come to recognize the movement, but the greatest fruits of the whole project are the thousands of lives being transformed by the power of the gospel. That's what collaboration is all about—to "preach Christ crucified (1 Cor 1:23)".

Opportunities to collaborate

Come and be a part of a missions' evangelistic project that will change the life of many nationals... and yours.

You could be one of those making a difference on our next mission's project.

Opportunities:

- Drama, arts, mime's presentations
- Lead a street evangelism team
- Be a counselor for new believers coming to Christ
- Children's ministry, clowns, puppets, musical, drama and art presentations
- Teach or work on a tent workshop for single mothers, fathers, addictions, etc...
- Minister at the youth tent and youth platform
- Musicians – Participate in the *Cultural Exchange*™
- Volunteers – Security team, ministry of help (ushers)
- Medical team – Physicians and Dentists to work on the *Humanitarian Mission* part of the festival

To receive a free collaboration brochure for the next mission, write to us to: **japerez.org/collaboration**

Testimonials

What I experienced could be the future of evangelism worldwide. Instead of one main evangelist, there were various working in their own specialties. The unity and camaraderie among the evangelists was an excellent example for the local church. To be able to have a city-wide effort, it is vital that everyone shelve their ego and work for the good of the Kingdom. JA Pérez was the first to do that (an excellent example of godliness), showing deference to the other evangelists who were there. This could be a prototype for the future! —*Dr. Jaime Mirón, General Editor of the Spanish translation of the Bible—the Nueva Traducción Viviente (NTV)*

JA Pérez models effective collaboration. He understands that one organization can do only so much, but through strategic partnerships and by working together, ministries can multiply their impact and reach far more people, far more cost-effectively for Jesus Christ. He has a lot of hands on experience in bringing together ministries with shared goals, values, and complementary gifts to positively impact cities in the name of Jesus. —*David L. Jones, Vice President of Corporate Affairs/Alliance Ministries, Luis Palau Association*

JA Pérez has come up with something that every outreach facilitator needs. He has a special way of incorporating the gifts of other pastors, evangelists, and fellow servants of the Lord as every minister has something different to add to the team. The heart of his ministry is to reach the lost, and to build unity in the cities reached. I believe the training and follow-up system the *JA Pérez Association* has implemented is extremely important and essential for the work of the Kingdom. I am excited to partner with JA Pérez and his wonderful team next year and the years to come. —**Alpha Hayward,** *Senior/Founding Pastor of Revolution Foursquare Church, and Founder of Day In The Park*

We are grateful to the *JA Pérez Association* for bringing the festival to our city. We the pastors have experienced a tremendous unity and believe the effects of the event will stay in the city long after the project has concluded with an extended impact reaching over 80,000 people. —**Pastor Jose Ramón Alvarado Arluvlu,** *Republic of Joy™ Festival Committee Member*

Collaborating with the *JA Pérez Association* has been an absolute blessing on so many levels. After serving with them in Mexico, Venezuela, Costa Rica and Haiti... not only have they made us feel like part of their family but we have made valuable friendships for life. JA Pérez and team are one of the most honest, hard working, loving, passionate and compassionate servants in evangelism I have ever met! Their events are always properly organized, the funds are meticulously maximized and responsibly managed, and safety in our travels is of utmost importance to them. The spiritual equipping, mentoring and encouragement before, during and after the trips are so valuable and have helped me and my ministry grow over the past several years. We have learned so much together, laughed so hard together and cried quite a bit together. *JA Pérez Association's* goal is always clear and present in every step of the way. When the *JA Pérez Team* comes into an area, the city impact begins months before the main event and continues for years after their team has left as they are not there to put on a "show", they go with every intention of making a permanent impact in the name of Jesus! Their ministry model is very effective. It is an absolute honor to have the opportunity to travel with them and share the BEST news ever...Jesus Christ is Lord! —*Georgina Verzal, Evangelist/Speaker Founder of Reg3neration™*

These have been two glorious festival days. For me personally, the greatest miracle of all has been to see the pastors together in unity... my heart rejoices, to see them all working together, sharing without rivalry... and enjoying the great blessing this event is bringing to the city. I'm grateful first to God and then to the team that collaborates with evangelist JA Pérez. Thank you, thank you, thank you for being such a blessing! — *Pastor Ana Aguirre, Republic of Joy™ Festival Committee Member*

We met JA Pérez back in November and were blessed when our city was chosen to host the festival. I thank God for the team of evangelists that came to work in an event of such great value—not only to our city but to the rest of Latin America. The festival has started a movement among the pastors as they have come to work together in the unity of the Spirit. I believe this is the beginning of a long term working relationship between the *Pérez Association* and the Pastor's Fraternity in this city. —*Pastor Josue Obando, Republic of Joy™ Festival, City Coordinator*

131

The model *JA Pérez Evangelist Association* uses is one that works. A team goes in advance to the site to coordinate the local churches and trains them to do counseling, door to door evangelism and promotion. Churches are then brought together to be trained collectively as the team builds up the body through messages from God's Word. As an evangelist and youth minister I would like to say that it was a blessing to work with JA Pérez and his team in Costa Rica. I saw God use the body of Christ to come together from all parts of the world as we worked to reach the people in the city. What one group, church or organization could never do alone was accomplished as God's Spirit moved on hearts and carried to one more region God's love and plan for the ages. *—Mark Johnston, Youth Evangelist/ Teacher/Youth Pastor at Bayside Church*

My opportunity to collaborate with JA Pérez and his team has been one of the best experiences in our ministry's short history. JA Pérez has implemented a model of collaboration for evangelists that benefits all involved. Whether your ministry is well seasoned and in a position to partner on a larger basis or if you're smaller and starting up, there's a place for you to serve, learn, and build God's kingdom together. JA Pérez is an outstanding evangelist, leader, and encourager of people. He has years of experience in evangelism ministry and is willing to build into you and your ministry. His entire team is a blessing to serve with and it's a fun time in fellowship while you're on the field. I highly recommend any collaborative opportunities with JA Pérez, you will not regret it. *—Paul Durham, Evangelist/ President, Ripe 4 Life Ministries*

Bringing the festival to our city represented an answer from God to our prayers. The impact this festival

132

has had over this city has been enormous in several dimensions; first with the local churches, where for the first time many pastors that had never participated in an event, came to work together; second the great unity among all leaders working together for the common good of the city; and thirdly, the massive number of people that have heard the message of the gospel—in every venue of the festival—and have responded to the call. We are grateful to the ministry of JA Pérez and all the other evangelists that came to our city and we give God all the glory for it. —*Pastor Randall Brenes, Vice President of Pastors Fraternity, Turrialba Costa Rica*

Collaboration is not only Biblical, it is powerful... When I have had the opportunity to collaborate with the *JA Pérez Association* I have always left encouraged and honored to be a part of a ministry that makes everyone feel included, where Jesus is the center! As it says in God's word, where two or more are gathered together, Jesus is in the midst! The Lord has used this ministry to reach thousands and the long term effect on a city is tremendous even after a collaborative event. This is only the catalyst that starts a movement of revival that cannot be stopped, as the Spirit of God continues to move changing a city forever. I have seen this first hand, after being a part of a festival that happened where we live and serve as missionaries, we are still seeing the effects today. —*Justin Benedict, Missionary Evangelist*

I noticed that at the JA Pérez outreach in Costa Rica, nobody spoke of their local denominational affiliation—all were there for one purpose. Thousands responded to the testimonies of changed lives as the team came together with the single purpose of sharing Christ—and him crucified. Working with so many evangelists and missionaries from all over the world,

133

and seeing the great work JA Pérez has been doing, has been a joy. May our work and what people like JA Pérez and others are doing permeate the world as we keep "making disciples from all nations". —*Raymond Centanni, Evangelist, Rock of Ages Festival Coordinator*

JA Pérez and the *JA Pérez Evangelistic Association* understand the value of working together in collaboration and the power that comes when sisters and brothers serve together to love God and love people. JA is a dynamic leader who selflessly yields the spotlight to others during speaking events. As he brings teams together, he strives to develop other speakers and leaders to become all that God has called them to be.

It has been an honor to serve with him and his team on several occasions for many reasons to include excellent organization, clear communication, flexibility on the ground during events, a team that serves with amazing hearts of love and patience as well as a passion to see people set free through The Gospel of Jesus Christ. This is anchored by a strong spiritual component that exudes the grace, power and favor of The LORD.

In my role in leadership development and the formation of strategic partnerships, I work with hundreds, maybe even thousands, of leaders in the field of evangelism and discipleship around the world. Everyone that I speak with supports JA's talents as a leader who can organize collaborative events. Partners report that serving with him in the field on location is a great joy as he serves tirelessly to maximize the time each team has in an area.

True leaders who follow the model and example of Jesus Christ give sacrificially and serve without

134

the expectation of fame, notoriety or praise. JA Pérez demonstrates this in organizing collaborative events with numerous evangelists and ministry partners of all expressions to include professional athletes, musicians and artists, teachers, speakers, humanitarian and medical, and much more. JA's strength is in developing others to their full potential through collaboration that empowers everyone who is involved with him and his team. Few leaders come along like this and I wholeheartedly endorse and support my dear brother JA Pérez in his collaborative efforts recommending anyone to partner with him as he leads teams to share and declare the good news of Jesus Christ.

—*Jeff Pieper* *Director of Strategic Relationships/Leadership Development, Luis Palau Association*

Other books by JA Pérez

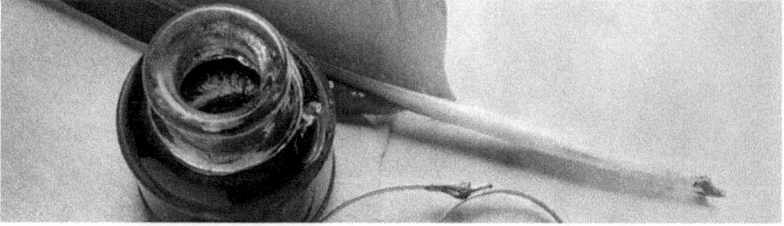

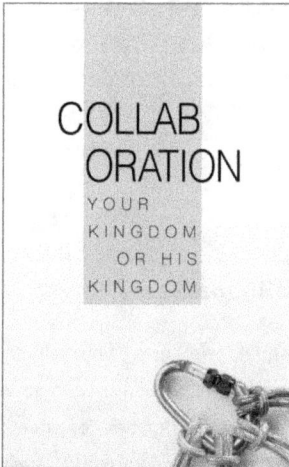

Collaboration: Your Kingdom or His Kingdom

Written in a factual, impactful style, this book exhibits the practices that make a collaborative venture succeed in a culturally-sensitive world. With his common sense and minimalist approach, the author presents core principles of partnership to help us accomplish the biblical mandate to reach the world for Christ.

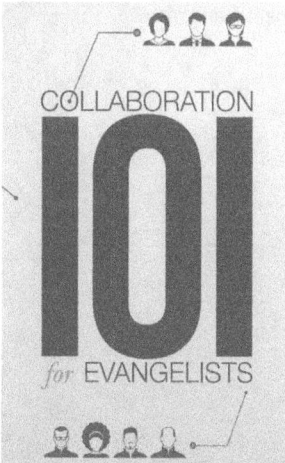

Collaboration 101 for Evangelists

The author presents principles of partnership and collaboration. Written specifically for Evangelists that want to work together to reach cities for Christ. You will find in this book why collaboration is the most cost-effective and practical way to do mass evangelism. Why you need others. Details on how to do international ministry, and where to start.

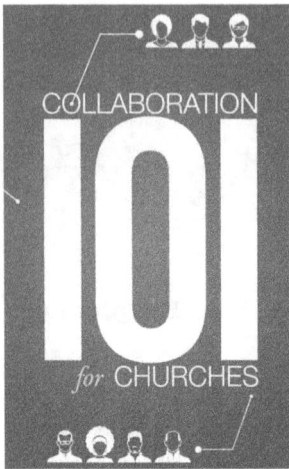

Collaboration 101 for Churches

When Pastors work together in a city-wide event, the impact is even greater. The author presents principles of partnership and collaboration. Written specifically for Pastors, Missionaries, and Church leaders that want to work together to reach cities for Christ. You will find in this book why collaboration is the most cost-effective and practical way to reach a city. Why you need others. The direct benefits of collaboration, and where to start.

Together: Collaborate

In this book/manual, we give you all the information you need to come with us and serve at a festival. Included: Opportunities for specific ministries, how our festival model works, travel information, application and more.

Books in Spanish

JA Pérez has written several books in the language of castilla—all available in Amazon.com and book stores worldwide. Books on the subjects of family, business, inspirational, poetry, devotionals, evangelism, and theology.

Latest Releases

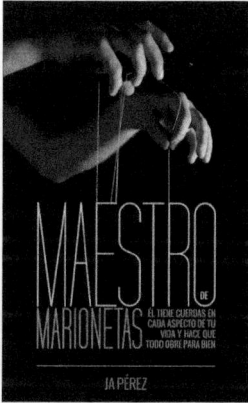

MAESTRO DE MARIONETAS
ÉL TIENE CUERDAS EN CADA ASPECTO DE TU VIDA Y HACE QUE TODO OBRE PARA BIEN
JA PÉREZ

GRACIA SOBERANA
SU SACRIFICIO fue SUFICIENTE
JA PÉREZ

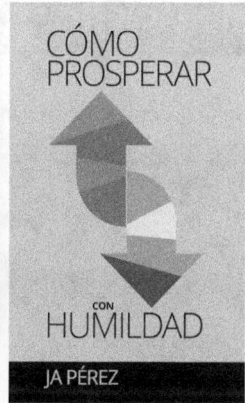

CÓMO PROSPERAR
CON HUMILDAD
JA PÉREZ

Devotionals

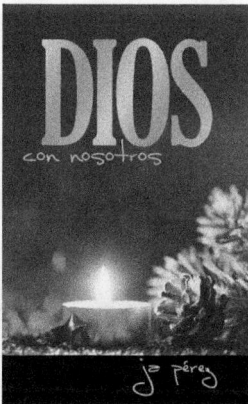

DIOS con nosotros
ja pérez

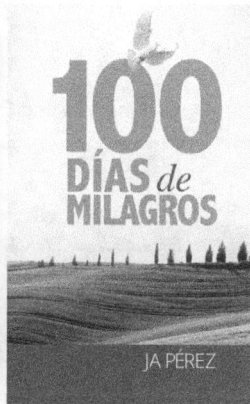

100 DÍAS de MILAGROS
JA PÉREZ

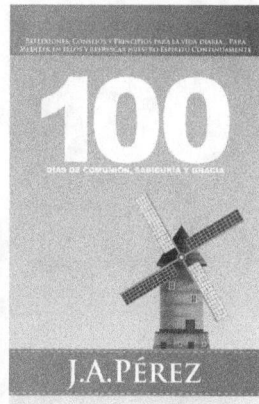

100 DÍAS DE COMUNIÓN, SABIDURÍA Y GRACIA
J.A. PÉREZ

On Inspiration and Creativity for Leadership

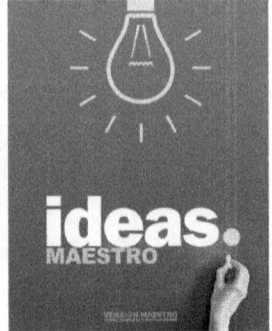

On Collaboration and Evangelism

On Finances and Economy

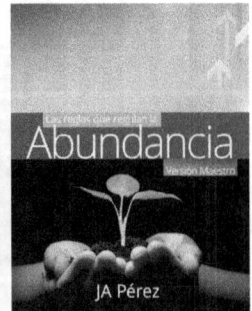

On Leadership and Government Diplomacy

On Discipleship and New Believer's Training

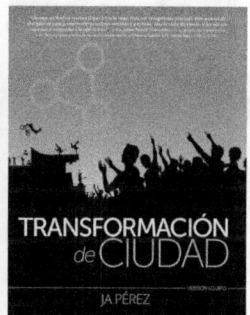

Books on Bible prophecy

On Christian Life, Growth, Life Principles, and Relationships

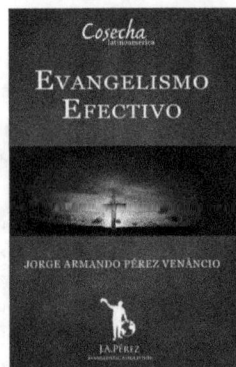

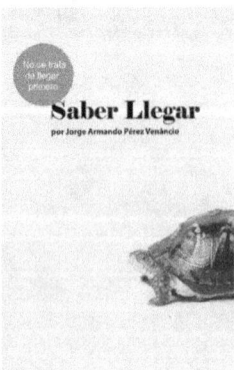

Contact / follow the author

Personal blog and social medias

japerez.org/blog

@japereznow

facebook.com/japereznow

JA Pérez Association

japerez.org

agenda@japerez.org

KEEN SIGHT BOOKS

www.ingramcontent.com/pod-product-compliance
Lightning Source LLC
LaVergne TN
LVHW051558080426
835510LV00020B/3033